Joan Bobkoff

Adelia Mostar

About the Authors

ELLEN BASS (left) offers lectures for survivors and their supporters and training seminars for counselors. For a schedule of upcoming events, please contact her through her Web site, www.ellenbass.com.

LAURA DAVIS offers lectures, workshops, and teleclasses (classes held over the phone) on reconciliation. She also has a free "Am I Ready to Reconcile?" e-zine and a free workbook available at www.LauraDavis.net.

The authors welcome any feedback or responses to *Beginning to Heal* but regret that they are unable to answer individual letters.

Ellen Bass and Laura Davis
P.O. Box 5296
Santa Cruz, CA 95063-5296

Beginning
to Heal

Also by the Authors

The Courage to Heal:
A Guide for Women Survivors of Child Sexual Abuse

Books by Ellen Bass

Mules of Love: Poems by Ellen Bass

Free Your Mind:
The Book for Gay, Lesbian, and Bisexual Youth—and Their Allies (coauthor)

I Never Told Anyone:
Writings by Women Survivors of Child Sexual Abuse (coeditor)

I Like You to Make Jokes with Me,
but I Don't Want You to Touch Me (for children)

Books and Tapes by Laura Davis

I Thought We'd Never Speak Again:
The Road from Estrangement to Reconciliation

The Last Frontier: Is Reconciliation Possible After Sexual Abuse?
(an audio/workbook set available at www.LauraDavis.net)

Becoming the Parent You Want to Be:
A Sourcebook of Strategies for the First Five Years (coauthor)

The Courage to Heal Workbook

Allies in Healing:
When the Person You Love Was Sexually Abused As a Child

Beginning to Heal

A First Book for Men and Women
Who Were Sexually Abused As Children

REVISED EDITION

Ellen Bass and Laura Davis

Quill

An Imprint of HarperCollinsPublishers

Although this book contains accounts from survivors of child sexual abuse, the names and/or other identifying characteristics of many of them have been changed to protect their privacy.

BEGINNING TO HEAL (Revised Edition). Copyright © 2003 by Ellen Bass and Laura Davis. All rights reserved. Printed in the United States of America. No part of this book may be used or reproduced in any manner whatsoever without written permission except in the case of brief quotations embodied in critical articles and reviews. For information address HarperCollins Publishers Inc., 10 East 53rd Street, New York, NY 10022.

HarperCollins books may be purchased for educational, business, or sales promotional use. For information please write: Special Markets Department, HarperCollins Publishers Inc., 10 East 53rd Street, New York, NY 10022.

A previous edition was published by HarperPerennial in 1993.
First Quill edition published 2003.

Designed by Elias Haslanger

Library of Congress Cataloging-in-Publication Data
Bass, Ellen.
  Beginning to heal : a first book for men and women who were sexually abused as children / Ellen Bass and Laura Davis.
    p. cm.
  ISBN 0-06-056469-5
    1. Adult child sexual abuse victims—United States—Psychology. 2. Child sexual abuse—United States. I. Davis, Laura, 1956– II. Title.

HV6570.2.B35 2003
362.76'4—dc21

2003049945

04 05 06 07 ❖/RRD 10 9 8 7 6 5 4 3 2

10/04

With deep appreciation, we thank all the survivors who so
generously shared their stories with us.

"There's more than anger, more than sadness, more than terror. There's hope."

—EDITH HORNING, SURVIVOR

"Why has it been worth it to heal? That's like asking, 'Why is it worth eating?' Because you die otherwise."

—DAVID CLOHESSY, SURVIVOR

"Don't give up. That's the best thing I could tell you. There are people who have lived through it, and as trite and stupid as it sounds to you right now, you will not be in so much pain later. If you made it this far, you've got some pretty good stuff in you. *Don't give up on yourself.*"

—CATHERINE, SURVIVOR

Contents

PART TWO **Stories of Courage**

A Letter to Our Readers

Dear Reader,

We wrote *Beginning to Heal* for men and women who are just starting to look at the issue of sexual abuse in their lives. *Beginning to Heal* will let you know you're not alone, and that there is a way out of the pain you're feeling. As you read, you may feel great relief. You may feel proud, strong, or able to make positive changes in your life.

But you may also feel afraid, angry, or deeply sad. If you have unfamiliar or upsetting feelings as you read, don't be alarmed. Strong feelings are part of healing.

If you don't have any feelings at all, that may mean you're not feeling safe enough yet to face the pain. That's okay. Take your time.

Reading this book is a little like healing itself. You don't have to go in a straight line, from beginning to end. Instead, go at your own pace, in your own way. You can skip chapters if you want to. Or read a page more than once. Make this book yours. It's okay to mark sections that are important to you or write notes to yourself in the margins.

If you come to a part of this book that's hard for you, you don't have to grit your teeth and keep reading. It's okay to stop, take a break, talk to someone about your feelings, and come back to it later. It's our hope that *Beginning to Heal* will offer you guidance and support, but it's not intended to take the place of therapy. Many survivors have found counseling to be a necessary part of their healing process.

We've expanded this new edition of *Beginning to Heal* to speak to men survivors of child sexual abuse, as well as to women, because we now know that the healing process is very much the same, no matter what your gender. We've also updated the book throughout to include our continuing learning about healing.

We wish you courage and support on your healing journey.

P.S. *Beginning to Heal* is drawn from our longer book, *The Courage to Heal*. We've made this book shorter and easier to read so more people can use it. When you're ready for a more thorough guide to healing, *The Courage to Heal* can offer a deeper level of support.

We also invite you to visit our Web sites for more information and resources. Ellen Bass is at www.ellenbass.com, and Laura Davis is at www.LauraDavis.net.

Part One

The Healing Process

Healing Is Possible

"There's nothing as wonderful as starting to heal, waking up in the morning and knowing that nobody can hurt you if you don't let them."

If you have been sexually abused, you are not alone. One out of three girls and one out of seven boys are abused by the time they reach eighteen. Sexually abused children come from every race, religion, and culture. They come from rich families and poor families. Abusers can be men or women, family members, friends, neighbors, teachers, counselors, priests or rabbis, baby-sitters, and strangers.

If you were abused as a child, you are probably still dealing with the effects in your life today. You may be having trouble at school, on the job, with relationships and sex, or in your family. You may feel bad about yourself or think something is wrong with you. These problems may be connected to the abuse you experienced while you were growing up.

The most important thing for you to know is that it is possible to heal from child sexual abuse. You don't have to live with the effects of abuse for the rest of your life. If you are willing to work hard and find good support, you can not only heal but thrive.

If you have been sexually abused,
you are not alone.

Was I Abused?

You've probably heard a lot about sexual abuse, but you may not be sure if your experience fits the definition.

Think back to when you were growing up. Did any of these things happen to you?

- Were you fondled or kissed in a way that felt bad to you?
- Were you ever touched unnecessarily on your private parts?
- Were you forced to touch someone else's private parts?
- Were you forced to have oral sex?
- Were you raped or was anything forced inside your vagina or anus?
- Were you forced to watch people have sex?
- Were you shown pornographic movies?
- Were you made to pose for sexual pictures?
- Were you made to sell your body for sex?
- Were you forced to abuse or hurt someone else?

If any of these things happened to you, then you were sexually abused.

Does My Experience Really Count?

Sometimes survivors think that what happened to them isn't bad enough to qualify as abuse. They say things like, "It wasn't incest— he was just a friend of the family," or "It only happened once," or

"It was just my brother and he was only a year older than me." But your pain counts.

The fact that someone else has suffered from abuse that was worse than yours does not lessen your suffering. The important thing in defining abuse is not the physical act that took place. It's how you felt as a child. An abuser used power to manipulate and control you. Your trust was shattered and the world stopped being safe. You felt terrified, hurt, ashamed, or confused.

Even abuse that isn't physical can leave deep scars. Your uncle walked naked around the house making sexual comments about your body. Your mother told you in detail about her sex life. These acts, though not directly physical, hurt you.

It doesn't matter how often you were abused. A father can stick his hand in his daughter's underwear in thirty seconds. After that the world is not the same.

The Healing Process

This book is about the healing process. Healing begins when you recognize that you were abused. And it leads to the satisfying experience of *thriving*.

> If you are willing to work hard and find good support, you can not only heal but thrive.

Survivors have taught us that there are recognizable stages in the healing process. This book will give you a map so you can see where you are, what you've already done, and what still lies ahead.

We've presented the stages of healing in a particular order, but you may not experience them that way. You may spend time focusing intensely on the abuse. Then your attention may shift more to your current life. When something in your life changes—you start a relationship, leave home, or have a child—you may deal with the abuse again, from a new vantage point. Each time, you learn more, feel more, and make more lasting changes.

> This book will give you a map of the healing process, so you can see where you are, what you've already done, and what still lies ahead.

The further along you are in the healing process, the more you'll be able to take care of yourself along the way. You'll be able to laugh, to experience pleasure along with the pain. You won't change your history, but it will no longer keep you from having a satisfying, full life.

There is no clear end to the healing process. It's a way of growing that continues throughout our lives.

You deserve this healing.

The Decision to Heal

"This has given me the opportunity to look at me. It's not all bad. You do heal. And you do become stronger. I don't know what it would take to flatten me, but it would have to be something really big. I am, in fact, a survivor."

The decision to heal from child sexual abuse is a powerful, positive choice. It is a commitment every survivor deserves to make. Healing can bring to your life a richness and depth you never dreamed possible:

> "For the first time, I'm appreciating things like the birds and the flowers, the way the sun feels on my skin—you know, really simple things. I can read a good book. I can sit in the sun. I don't ever remember enjoying these things, even as a little kid. I've woken up. If this hadn't happened, I'd still be asleep. So for the first time, I feel alive. And you know that's something to go for."

Survivors decide to heal for many different reasons. Some say they were "falling apart at the seams" or "hitting bottom." Others are motivated by changes in their lives. A young girl turns her step-father in for molesting her and the judge sends her to therapy. A young man finds himself unable to stay close to his girlfriend once they get married. A mother starts having terrible nightmares when her daughter reaches the age she was when the abuse began. A man reads a news report about a group of boys abused by a popular coach and can't stop thinking about his own abuse. An alcoholic quits drinking and starts having troubling memories from child-hood.

> The decision to heal from child sexual abuse is a powerful, positive choice.

What Is It Like to Heal?

Once you decide to face your abuse, you probably want to heal as quickly as possible. Unfortunately, healing doesn't work that way. Lasting change takes time.

It is always worth it to heal. But it is rarely easy. Deciding to heal can lead to serious conflicts with people you care about. You may find it hard to study, work, take care of your children, or even make dinner. You may be unable to sleep, eat, or stop crying:

> "If I'd known anything could hurt this much or be this sad, I never would have decided to heal. And at the same time you can't go back. You can't sweep it back under the rug."

There will probably be times when you wonder if healing is worth it. But as one survivor put it, "Taking that risk was the most promising choice I had."

It is scary to face the unknown. But it is a tremendous relief to stop running away from the pain:

> "There is comfort in knowing that you don't have to pretend anymore, that you are going to do everything within your power to heal."

It is a tremendous relief to stop running away from the pain.

Don't Try to Do It Alone

You can't heal from child sexual abuse alone. You need to break the silence that has surrounded the abuse and reach out for support.

At least one person needs to know about your pain and your healing. That person can be a friend, counselor, spouse or partner, fellow survivor, or family member. We hope that you will have many people who support you. But start with one person. Find someone you trust and talk about it.

The Emergency Stage

"I felt like I was standing in a room, looking at the floor. I was shattered all over it. I was picking up pieces of my life and looking at them, saying, 'Do I want to keep this? Is this of any use to me anymore? When will the pain stop?'"

Many survivors go through a period when sexual abuse is all they think about. We call it the emergency stage. You talk about the abuse to anyone who will listen. You think about it all day and have nightmares at night. Your life is full of crises. You can't stop crying, and it's hard to function. As one man recalled:

"There was a time when I'd get up in the morning, I'd shave and shower, eat my breakfast, and get dressed. Then, half the time, I couldn't walk out the front door."

People often describe the early stages of their healing as a natural disaster: "It was like being caught in an avalanche." "It was like an earthquake."

Here's how one woman experienced the emergency stage:

"It was like there were large six-foot-high letters in my living room every day when I woke up: INCEST! I felt everyone knew I was an incest victim. I thought I looked like one.

"I had no energy to deal with other people or their problems. My reserves had been drained. For a long time, all I cared about was going to sleep and being able to wake up the next day.

"I had to find people who would sit with me no matter how I felt. I had one friend who'd been beaten when she was a kid. She understood. I could call her when I felt horrible, and she'd let me come over to just eat and watch TV.

"I also had to find a safe place to be alone. I went for walks in the woods. I ran a lot. I'd go for twenty-mile bike rides.

"The only thing that saved me when I felt totally cut off was that I had my therapist's phone number written all over my house. I had it on the mirror in the bathroom. I had it in my journal. I had it in books I was reading. I burned it in my memory, so at any time I could call her. Many times, just making the call and getting her answering machine, and being able to leave a message in my cracking, crying voice, let me know I could reach out. I knew she would call me eventually, and I could hold out till then.

"After a year, I was able to lift my head up a little bit and notice that the season had changed. I started to realize that even though I was an incest survivor, I could go on with my life. That was a tremendous relief."

Surviving the Emergency Stage

The most important thing to remember about the emergency stage is that it will end. There will be a time when you will not be thinking about sexual abuse twenty-four hours a day. Until then, *your job is to take care of yourself and to keep yourself safe.*

- **Don't try to hurt or kill yourself.** You survived the abuse and you can survive the healing process, too. (See the box on page 13.)
- **Remind yourself that you're not going crazy.** You're going through a natural part of the healing process.
- **Find people you can talk to.** And get support from other survivors.
- **Allow yourself to think about the abuse as much as you need to.** And when you're able to focus on other things, take advantage of the break.
- **Drop any responsibilities that aren't essential.**
- **Don't use alcohol or drugs to stop the pain.** Numbing your feelings will only make the crisis last longer.
- **Get out of dangerous or abusive situations.** If you are in an abusive relationship, if your children are in danger, or if someone is still sexually abusing you, get the help you need to leave. Call the National Child Abuse Hotline at 1-800-422-4453. Or visit their Web site at www.childhelpusa.org.
- **Sit tight and ride out the storm.** Your thinking isn't that clear right now. Unless you're in danger, this is not usually a good time to make major life changes.
- **Develop a belief in something greater than yourself.** Spirituality can give you hope and strength.
- **Talk to people who are further along in their healing.**
- **Do as many nice things for yourself as possible.**

Don't Kill Yourself

Sometimes you feel so bad that you don't want to live. The pain is too great. You hate yourself and feel afraid. You want to die.

These are your real feelings. Don't deny them. But don't act on them. *Don't kill yourself.*

We have lost far too many survivors already. Too many victims—children, teenagers, and adults—have lacked support and hope, and out of despair have killed themselves. We can't afford to lose you. You deserve to live.

Read the chapter on anger. When you feel so bad you want to die, you need to focus your anger toward the people who hurt you, not at yourself. As you direct your anger where it belongs, your self-hate will lessen. You will want to live.

This takes time. Right now, get help. If the first person you call isn't helpful, try someone else. Make a list of support people and their phone numbers. If you start feeling like you want to hurt yourself, call them. If you don't know whom to call, call the operator and ask to be connected to a suicide prevention hotline. A call to them can save your life.

You may feel like you can't stand it another minute. But the feelings will pass. You can learn to wait them out.

Each time you bear the pain of your feelings without hurting yourself, you become stronger. Each time you reach out for help, you defeat your abusers. You have not let them destroy you.

The most important thing to remember about the emergency stage is that it will end. Until then, your job is to take care of yourself and to keep yourself safe.

Tips for Dealing with Panic

Panic is what you feel when your feelings seem out of control. You're scared. Your heart is pounding. You can't catch your breath. The fear keeps getting stronger. You want to run away.

Panic attacks can be caused by triggers—things in the present that remind you of times you were terrified in the past.

When you start to feel panicky, don't rush into action. Don't drive. Don't drink or abuse drugs. Don't hurt yourself or anyone else. Acting out of panic leads to poor choices.

To calm yourself down, do whatever works that keeps you and others safe. One survivor explained:

> "I try to breathe, but it's the hardest thing to do when I feel that way. I try to get out in nature, away from people. I find nature very calming. I get myself out in the trees and just breathe."

Another survivor finds it helpful to sit quietly and observe what's going on in the moment:

> "I pay attention to the sensations in my body: My throat is feeling tight; my heart is racing; I feel pressure in my belly. I watch my thoughts: *I want to jump up and do something—anything—to make these feelings go away.* When I'm able to observe what is happening inside me,

it starts to change. And I realize that there is more to me
that just the panic I'm feeling."

When you're not feeling scared, make a list of things that help
you relax. The next time you panic, pick up your list and do the
thing at the top of the list. Then work your way down.

Everyone's list will be different. But be sure you include the
phone numbers of people you can call. When you're feeling scared,
it's often the hardest time to reach out. Do it anyway.

A sample list might look like this:

Things to Do During a Panic

1) Breathe.
2) Take a brisk walk.
3) Call Jim *(Write the phone numbers on your list)*.
4) Call Nona if Jim's not home. Go down my list of support people and keep calling.
5) Write in my journal.
6) Take a hot bath.
7) Write a hundred times, *I'm safe. They can't hurt me
   anymore.*
8) Go for a run, or exercise.
9) Listen to soothing music.
10) Meditate, pray, or do yoga.
11) Draw a picture of how I feel.
12) Watch an old movie on TV.
13) Eat tomato soup or grilled cheese.
14) Start again at the top.

If all else fails, sit in a chair, put your hands in your lap or rest
your arms on the armrest, and just stay there. You may have a mis-

erable night, but in the morning, you won't have done any damage. Then you can try to reach out for help again.

> When you're feeling scared, it's often the hardest time to reach out. Do it anyway.

What Gives Me Hope

This is what some survivors told us:

"My friend Patricia gave me hope. She would basically talk me into wanting to live."

"The thing that gives me hope is remembering what my therapist kept saying to me, over and over, 'This is part of the change process.' I held on to that when there was really nothing else to hold on to."

"I got a lot of hope from the men in my support group."

"I was once a nun in a contemplative order. Because I had lived that lifestyle, I knew things took a long time. I knew that the process of becoming holy, of knowing God, was very slow. Day by day, I just knew I was growing closer to God. It was the same with the incest. I just trusted that something was happening, that there was a hidden growth going on."

"My brother inspires me through his struggle. He had it a lot worse than I did, and he is struggling to live."

"Helping others speak out gives me hope."

"Every time I heal a little bit more, I'm able to give my children a better childhood. I become a better father to them."

"My own inner strength gives me hope. I just won't quit. Period."

> "My own inner strength gives me hope. I just won't quit. Period."

Remembering

"I've looked the memories in the face and smelled
their breath. They can't hurt me anymore."

The experience of remembering abuse varies greatly from survivor to survivor. Many people have always remembered their abuse. They may have minimized its importance, denied its impact on their lives, or been numb to their feelings, but they have never forgotten the events themselves. One survivor explained:

> "I could rattle off the facts of my abuse like a grocery list, but remembering the fear and terror and pain was another matter entirely."

Some people recall just part of what happened to them. They remember beatings or humiliation, but not the sexual assaults that went with them. They remember the exam in the hospital emergency room—but not the rape that preceded it.

There are also survivors who don't remember anything about their abuse until the memories come crashing through. A change in your life or a particular event can bring up memories that have been buried for years:

"If he hadn't confessed, I might never have remembered. I'd repressed it so completely. It was just a matter of survival. But going underground like that has its price. When the memories flooded back in, I collapsed. I thought I had it all together. I was a hard-working husband, a good father, and a decent athlete—but it was all a house of cards."

Forgetting the abuse and then remembering it later is a survival tool that makes sense. You forget until it's safe enough to remember. Your mind protects you.

The fact that you're remembering now means that you're ready to learn about your history.

> Forgetting the abuse and then remembering it later is a survival tool that makes sense.

What Remembering Is Like

The process of remembering is like putting together a jigsaw puzzle. Memories often come back in bits and pieces. They can seem distant, like something you're observing from far away, or as clear as a snapshot:

"I'd be driving and I'd start having flashes of things— like bloody sheets, or taking a bath, or throwing away my nightgown. For a long time, I remembered all the things around being raped but not the rape itself."

You may have flashbacks in which you relive experiences you had as a child. Flashbacks are memories that are so vivid that you feel as though the original experience is happening again *now*, rather than just being remembered. You smell the abuser's breath. You see the room you slept in as a child. You feel the terror you felt as a six-year-old.

Most of us expect memories to be visual. But they're not always that way. One woman was held facedown on the seat of a car and raped by her father. She didn't *see* anything. But she heard him. And when she began to write about it in Spanish, her native language, it all came back.

You may also remember with your body. Your wife touches you and you feel disgusted. After sex you feel dirty and ashamed. You don't have specific pictures, but your body remembers the abuse.

Letting Memories In

Some survivors go through a time in which they are flooded with memories from the past. If this is happening to you, don't try to push the memories away. If you do, you may end up exhausted, or plagued by headaches, panic attacks, or nightmares. Usually it's best to just let the memories come through.

- **Find a place where you'll be safe.**
- **Call a support person if you want to be with someone.** Or you might prefer being alone.
- **Don't fight it.** Relax and let the memory come. Don't use drugs, alcohol, or food to push it down.
- **Remember, it's just a memory.** Your abuser is not really hurting you now, even if it feels that way. Remembering is part of healing. It's not more abuse.
- **Expect to have a response.** It's painful and draining to remember. It may take you a while to recover.

- **Nurture yourself.** You need extra comfort and care right now.
- **Tell at least one other person.** You suffered alone as a child. You don't have to do that again.

As you remember, it's important to let yourself feel. Yet that's very hard to do. When you remember the terror, the physical pain, and the panic, the feelings can be as intense as the actual experience:

> "I found myself slipping into the feelings I'd had dur-
> ing the abuse. There was this tremendous isolation. I got
> in touch with how frightening the world is. It was the
> worst of the fear finally coming up. I felt like it was
> right at the top of my neck all the time, ready to come
> out in a scream."

Having to experience the feelings is one of the hardest parts of remembering. Yet it can also bring relief:

> "The more I heal, the more I see these memories are
> literally stored in my body, and they've got to get out.
> Otherwise I'm going to carry them forever."

Remembering is part of healing. It's not more
abuse.

How Can I Know If My Memories Are Real?

Not all memories are completely accurate. They show us how we felt at the time, but the events may not have occurred exactly the way we remember them.

One survivor had always remembered the abuser putting a knife in her vagina. But she went on to explain that she didn't think that's what actually happened. There was no blood, no scarring, and she had no memory of the actual knife. After consideration, she came to the conclusion that the abuser must have penetrated her vagina—perhaps with a finger or his penis—and the feeling was so painful, so sharp and cutting, that she, in her child's mind, had no way to explain it, other than as a knife.

The way this woman worked with her memories is a good model. If you're not sure what happened to you, don't jump to conclusions or let anyone pressure you one way or the other. As one woman relates, not all bad experiences are sexual abuse:

> "I grew up in a very abusive home. My mother had three husbands who beat her, and they beat us, too. Violence and drinking were a part of our daily life and I never forgot a bit of it. Years later, when I was trying to heal, people kept insisting that I'd been sexually abused. But it just didn't ring true for me. Finally I realized what I'd been through was bad enough to cause the problems in my life. Although a lot of crummy stuff happened to me, sexual abuse wasn't part of it."

Although uncertainty can be frustrating, try to be patient and trust that over time you'll be able to sort out your past. One man recalled:

> "When I heard about abuse in the church, I got these really creepy feelings. I started to sweat and felt this terrible anxiety. I had weird flashes of images from choir practice when I was a boy. The memories were so sketchy I couldn't put much stock in them. Part of me

thought that something had happened to me, and the other part was sure that I was just being influenced by what I heard on the news. Then I got the call. My brother phoned to tell me that our old minister had just been arrested for molesting three boys. After that, I knew."

Continue to explore your feelings and your history. Take your time and eventually things will become clearer.

Believing It Happened

"I did not want to believe with a passion. Even as part of me recognized the truth, another part fought to deny it. There were times when I would rather have viewed myself as crazy than acknowledge what had happened to me."

Some survivors have no trouble believing they were abused. You may have a sibling who was there. A mother who says, "But honey, I had to stay with him." An abuser who admits it. But even survivors who have proof of their abuse sometimes struggle to believe it really happened.

For many survivors, denial has been a way of life. You may have grown up in a family where many things were denied, not just abuse. You may have learned to numb your feelings or ignore painful realities. These patterns don't just disappear, even when there's clear proof of abuse.

To heal, we have to face the truth. Yet often this is difficult. When children are abused, it becomes dangerous for them to trust their own perceptions. You couldn't admit that the same neighbor who taught you to ride a bike also made you touch his penis. That was just too horrible to bear. So you pretended it didn't happen.

One of the most common ways people deal with hurt is denial. Children sometimes go to great lengths to deny their own abuse:

> "When my father would come into my room at night, I'd think, *That's not my father. That's an alien being. Invaders have taken over his body.*"

If the adults around you told you that your experiences didn't happen, you may have become confused and unsure about what was real. Your brother said he was just tucking you in. Your stepfather told you it was for your own good. Your mother said you were dreaming. Your uncle said, "You're crazy. No one will ever believe you."

It's not just family members who deny abuse. Teachers, doctors, counselors, and ministers sometimes do, too. They say things like, "But your grandfather is a deacon in the church," or, "You should be over that by now."

And of course, you don't want it to be true. No wonder so many survivors struggle to believe that the abuse really happened.

One of the most common ways people deal with hurt is denial. We pretend it never happened.

Believing Doesn't Happen All at Once

Even when you know the facts are true, you may still, at a deep emotional level, have trouble believing that your abuse mattered. One man recalled:

> "I built up such a hard exterior. I never showed any real emotion. I never told anyone what I had experienced as

a child. I always remembered the abuse, but I denied that it hurt me."

Abuse always hurts us. But sometimes it takes quite a while to recognize the impact it has had on our lives. As we come to believe that the abuse really did happen and that it mattered, we begin to accept it as part of our lives:

"For a long time, I thought of the abuse as something that had happened to someone very far away from me. Over time I've been able to incorporate it more into the texture of my life. I talk about it freely, much as I would the fact that my family went to museums a lot when I was a kid. I used to feel I had this good childhood, and then off to the side was this horrible, shameful abuse. But now I know there was only one child, and she lived through it all."

To heal, you have to face the truth.

Breaking Silence

"You know how they say, 'Speak the truth and the truth shall set you free.' Well, that's how it really is. I'm not in a cage anymore. There are no more secrets. And it's the secrets that kill you."

To heal from child sexual abuse, you need to tell the truth about your life. Although most survivors have been taught to keep the abuse a secret, this silence has been in the best interests of the abusers, not the survivors.

Many survivors want to speak out. Yet each time you consider breaking the taboo of secrecy, you are bound to feel fear and confusion. This is because you are fighting against a system that wants to keep you powerless and silent.

How You Were Silenced

As a child, you might not have told anyone about the abuse. You may have felt ashamed or thought it was your fault. You may have been afraid you'd be punished or that people would think you were bad.

Your abuser may have said, "I'll kill you if you tell," or "You'll be put in jail." If you did get up the nerve to talk, telling may have led to further abuse.

In an ideal world, you would have been believed and comforted. But this may not have happened. Instead, you may have been blamed, punished, or called a liar.

Or your story may have been met with silence. No one talked about it. You were told never to bring it up again. You got the message that your experience was too horrible for words and, perhaps, that you were too horrible. You learned it wasn't safe to tell the truth. In this way, you learned shame, secrecy, and silence. One man reflected:

> "One of the hardest things for me as a man looking back on my childhood is that my voice got taken away. I never shouted and said, 'You can't do that.' I stayed quiet. I never said a word. I never told my mom what was happening.
>
> "When I see empowered children today, it blows my mind. It also makes me feel sad. I wish I could have learned to say, 'No!' It would have helped me a lot, but I never got that skill."

Telling Takes a Leap of Faith

When you first tell someone that you were sexually abused, you may feel both terrified and relieved. Then you may wonder if you've done the right thing. It's scary, and the results are uncertain, but it's important to talk about the abuse. Telling someone has many benefits:

- You face the truth about your abuse.
- You can get help.
- You get more in touch with your feelings.
- You see your experience through the eyes of a person who cares.
- You create deeper, more honest relationships.
- You join a courageous group of survivors who refuse to suffer in silence.
- You help end abuse by breaking the silence in which it thrives.
- You are a model for other survivors.
- You (eventually) feel proud and strong.

> To heal from child sexual abuse, you need to tell
> the truth about your life.

Choosing Someone to Tell

When you first begin talking about your abuse, start with people who are likely to respond well. Begin with the person you trust the most. That might be a counselor, a friend, or your spouse or partner.

A survivors' support group can also be an excellent place to tell your story. As you listen to other survivors, you realize you're not alone. And when it's your turn to talk, you experience the understanding and caring of the group:

> "The last thing on earth I wanted to do was sit around with a group of men talking about what happened to me as a kid. It was hard enough for me to tell one person how depressed and incapacitated I felt, much less sit in a room and tell seven people.
>
> "But when I finally went to group therapy, I saw all these people who'd gone through even more than I did,

and they were making headway. That was always very inspiring to me."

But letting people know what you're really going through can be scary or make you feel vulnerable:

> "It's been relatively easy for me to talk about what happened to me as a child. It's much more difficult to talk about the effects in my adulthood. For me to talk about my sexual problems or control issues is a lot harder."

Yet being honest with the people closest to you is important. Your friends need to understand why you're upset or why it's hard for you to trust. Your partner needs to know why you're distant or want sex all the time or not at all. Sharing your real feelings is the first step in getting the support you need.

If you're thinking of telling someone, ask yourself:

- Does this person love and respect me?
- Have we been able to talk about personal things before?
- Does this person care about how I feel?
- Do I trust this person?
- Do I feel safe with this person?

If you can answer yes to these questions, you're choosing someone who's likely to support you.

Pick a time when neither of you has to rush. And if you want your friend not to tell anyone, be sure to say so.

At the end of this book, on page 93, "For Supporters of Survivors" can help people understand how to respond to you in a helpful way. You might want to ask your friend to read it before you share your story.

When you tell someone and they listen with
respect and caring, your life changes dramatically.

Reactions to Telling

It's an honor to listen to the truth of someone's life. When you
share difficult truths with someone, they should respect that telling.
But that doesn't always happen. Some people are threatened by the
whole idea of child sexual abuse. Your story may remind them of
things they're not ready to deal with. People may withdraw or get
angry. Some people won't believe you. Others will insist you "get
over it." You may even lose some friends or family members who
can't deal with your honesty.

Hostile or negative reactions are painful, of course. But other
relationships will grow deeper.

To heal from sexual abuse, you need relationships in which you
can be your whole self—with your history and your pain. The only
way to create those relationships is to share honestly.

It's an honor to listen to the truth of someone's life.

Understanding That It Wasn't Your Fault

"I know I was only five years old, but I was an extremely intelligent five-year-old. I should have been able to figure out a way to escape."

Most children blame themselves for being sexually abused. Many adult survivors continue to blame themselves. But sexual abuse is *never* the fault of the child.

There are many reasons you may blame yourself for the abuse. The abuser may have told you it was your fault. Your friend's father said, "You're such a sexy little girl, I can't keep my hands off you." Your brother confused you by asking, "You really want to be close to me, don't you?"

You may have been punished if you told. Or called a liar. Your religion may have told you that you were a sinner and that you'd go to hell for the things your mother was making you do. One woman said:

"I felt like I was really evil. It's like those child-devil movies. Inside this innocent little child is this evil seed. I used to think I made people feel bad and made bad things happen."

As a child, it was too scary to believe that the adults around you were out of control. If you blamed yourself, there was a chance you could fix things by being good. In a strange way, blaming yourself gave you hope.

Survivors blame themselves because they took money, gifts, or special favors. But if you were able to get some small thing back, give yourself credit. One woman was given a bicycle by her abuser. She was able to ride the bicycle into the woods and feel safe. She blamed herself for taking it. Instead she should be praised for finding a way to escape.

Sexual abuse is *never* the fault of the child.

But I Should Have Been Able to Stop It

Many survivors blame themselves for not stopping the abuser. One man recalled:

> "My brother made me give him oral sex. It started when I was six and lasted until I was sixteen. At first I thought it was normal. But later, when I said I didn't want to, he beat me up. That's when I realized it was wrong. But I felt so bad about myself, I wasn't capable of telling anyone.
>
> "I felt a tremendous amount of shame because I hadn't stuck up for myself. I felt shame for being so vulnerable, shame for sucking another guy's dick.
>
> "Like every boy, I was taught that boys should never cry or show fear or be taken advantage of.
>
> "But I was shy. I was submissive. I cried. I did whatever my brother wanted me to do. Everything males

strive to be, I wasn't. I felt helpless and hopeless, and I believed it was all my fault."

But the abuse was not your fault. As a child, you didn't have the resources you have now.

But I Wanted to Be Close

You may feel ashamed because you wanted to be close to the abuser. You needed attention and affection. You weren't getting it anywhere else. So you didn't fight off the sexual advances. Survivors say, "But I'm the one who asked for the back rub," or "I climbed into his bed."

But you were not wrong. Every child needs attention and affection. If they are not offered in healthy ways, children will take them in whatever way they can, because they are essential needs.

Every child needs attention and affection.

But It Felt Good

Some children only feel pain and anguish while they're being abused. But others experience pleasure in their bodies. If the abuse felt good or if you had an orgasm, you may feel particularly ashamed. One woman explained:

"Some of it felt good, and ugh! It's still hard for me to talk about it. When I think back on times I was close to my mother in a sexual way, where I was getting turned on, there's a lot of shame there. It feels really embarrassing."

One survivor was gang-raped as a teenager and had an orgasm. "For a long time I thought it was a cruel joke that God had made my body that way." She desperately needed to know that she wasn't the only survivor who'd had an orgasm while being abused.

A man who was abused by his priest had to work hard to overcome the shame:

> "He would finish with me and I would pull up my pants. The sensation of wetness was a horrible reminder of what I'd been through. Something had been ejected from my body that I couldn't take back. Even though the abuse always happened behind closed doors, I felt exposed to the world. I'd leave the rectory, hop on my bike, and pedal as fast as I could to get away.
>
> "A tremendous pool of shame built up inside me. It filled fuller and fuller, until I was drowning.
>
> "Talking about the details has helped me get over the shame. Every time I talk about the abuse, I'm emptying another gallon out of that pool of shame."

It is natural to have sexual feelings when we are touched in a sexual way. If you had an orgasm when you were abused, it doesn't mean you wanted the abuse. Your body simply did what bodies are supposed to do. Your body didn't betray you. The abuser did.

Overcoming Shame

There are many ways to overcome shame. One of the most powerful is talking to a trusted person about your abuse:

"A key sign of healing is that your shame becomes less. Instead of looking at someone's watch while you tell them what happened, you can look at their face. And then eventually you can look in their eyes and tell them, without feeling they can see what a creep you are."

Being in a group with other survivors is also a powerful way to overcome shame. When you hear other survivors tell their stories, you can see the goodness in them. When they listen to you with the same concern and respect, you start to see yourself as a proud survivor who was not to blame. As one woman put it, "When your counselor says, 'It wasn't your fault,' that's one thing. But when you have eight people saying it to you, it's a lot more powerful."

Speaking out in public can be another way to transform shame into a feeling of power. Many survivors choose to work with abused children, educate the public, or work to make the justice system more responsive to children's needs.

Spending time with children can also give you strong evidence that the abuse wasn't your fault. Children remind you how small and powerless you were when you were young. One mother talked about her daughter:

> "When I saw how little power she had, how small she was when I put her to bed, I got a real picture of how small and vulnerable *I* had been. I got it in my heart that abuse was not okay. And that I had not been responsible for what had happened to me. I started to forgive myself."

No matter how old you were, no matter what the situation was, there is never an excuse for sexual abuse. If you were abused, it was not your fault.

The Child Within

"I've taken out old pictures and stared at them
deeply, trying to look into the eyes of myself as a
child. I imagine the scenes I went through. I find
quiet moments when I can reflect on him. I talk
about him. I keep him alive inside me."

Inside all of us, we carry the feelings and the hurts we felt as children. They may be buried, but they are still there. In order to heal, we need to get in touch with these lost parts of ourselves.

The abuse happened when we were young. It is the child inside you who holds the key to our memories and feelings.

When you were a child, you had to hide vulnerability. Being asked to remember it now can feel threatening. It means remembering your shame and terror. It means remembering a time when you did not have the power to protect yourself.

Many survivors blame or ignore that child. You hate yourself for having been small, for having needed affection, for having "let yourself be abused." But when you hate the child inside you, you hate a part of yourself. When you take care of the child inside, you learn to nurture yourself.

The child inside you holds the key to your
memories and feelings.

Connecting with the Child Within

One man made a conscious effort to think about himself as a child:

> "I go back and try to remember what it was like when
> I was nine or ten, lying in bed at night, looking up at
> the ceiling. What were my thoughts? How did I man-
> age all the confusion I was going through? I reconnect
> with that child. I say to myself, 'He's innocent and he's
> right inside of me.'"

Another survivor gained sympathy for herself as a child while
handing out Halloween candy:

> "I have always loved children, but for months after I
> remembered the incest, it was too painful to be around
> them. I'd see them playing or running down the street,
> little girls flipping up their skirts and showing white cot-
> ton panties. I'd cringe inside. *They're too vulnerable.*
>
> "I spent Halloween at my friend's house, just a few
> months after I had my first memories. The doorbell
> rang. I opened the door to a mother and little girl. The
> girl was dressed as an angel, in a flowing white dress
> with gold trim. She had straight blond hair cut in a
> pageboy. Set on her head was a halo made of aluminum
> foil and a bent wire coat hanger. I asked her how old
> she was. 'Five and a half,' she said proudly.

"I couldn't take my eyes off her. She looked exactly like I had when I was her age. It was like looking back twenty-five years. I stared at her until her mother glared at me. I gave the girl a Snickers bar and turned away. I slowly shut the door and sat down in the living room, dazed.

"All I could think was, *That's how young I was! I was that little when he forced himself on me. How could he have done that?* I felt tears of outrage and grief. I had been innocent! There was nothing I could have done to protect myself. None of it had been my fault. 'I was only a child,' I screamed into the empty living room, the sudden reality of a child of five flooding through me."

Rewards You Didn't Expect

Getting in touch with the child inside means facing that child's pain and terror and offering comfort in the night. It also can bring you rewards you didn't expect:

"I was much too scared when I was a child to ever let loose and enjoy being a kid. Now I'm making up for lost time. I'm learning to be silly and to play and to not be so serious all the time."

Get to know the child inside you. You may discover a freer, more playful side of yourself.

When you take care of the child inside, you learn to nurture yourself.

Grieving

"Sometimes I think I'm going to die from the sadness. Not that anyone ever died from crying for
two hours, but it sure feels like it."

As a survivor of child sexual abuse you have a lot to grieve for.
You grieve for the ways you were hurt. You grieve for not being
protected, for the things you missed out on as a child. You grieve
for the time and effort it takes to heal, for the relationships and
happiness you have lost.

You may have to grieve for your lost faith or give up the idea
that the abuser had your best interests at heart.

You may have to grieve for the fact that you don't have suitable
grandparents for your children, or a family you can depend on.

You must also grieve for the shattered image of a world that is
fair and safe for children. You will grieve for your lost innocence
and ability to trust.

As a survivor of child sexual abuse you have a lot
to grieve for.

Buried Grief

Buried grief poisons you. It limits your ability to feel joy or to be fully alive. An important part of healing is to express the grief you've carried inside.

When you were young, you had to hide your feelings. Now, to move on in your life, you have to feel the grief and anguish, but this time with the support of caring people. You might wonder how going back into the pain can help release you from it. But this is how healing from trauma works. One man experienced it this way:

> "It feels like there is a barrier halfway down my body. My feelings are in my stomach area and there are walls keeping them there. Once in a while, feelings slip through, but mostly, the walls keep everything under control.
>
> "When the walls give way, I am in a sea of feelings. It's hard, but I now know that I'm never going to heal without those feelings."

The way to move beyond grief is to experience your pain fully and honor your feelings. When you face your feelings, and they are met with caring and compassion, they change.

About Grief

You may feel foolish crying over events that happened so long ago. But grief stays stored up until you have a chance to express it:

> "There were times I'd have to cry into the pillow because I was just wailing. I'd be crying so hard that I

could hardly breathe. I'd cry like that for an hour. I remember thinking, 'This is never going to end. They're going to have to come lock me up. I'll never be able to pull myself out of this.'

"My wife would lie there and hold me. When it was finally over, I'd take a shower and we'd have to change the sheets on the bed because it was soaked. Afterwards, I'd feel exhausted and relieved—relieved that it was over, but fearful because I never knew when the next bout would be."

The way to move beyond grief is to experience your pain fully and honor your feelings.

Grief has its own timing. You can't say, "This is it. I'm going to grieve now." You have to make room for grief as it arises. You need to give yourself the time and space to let go:

"I had been in therapy for several months and I began to feel safe. There were weeks when I entered the building, went up the stairs, and checked in, all with a smile on my face. Then I'd enter the office, and my therapist would close the door. Before she could even get to her chair, I'd be crying. Deep within me I held those feelings, waiting until I knew there would be time and compassion."

However you grieve, allow yourself to release the feelings you've been holding inside. Grieving can be a great relief.

Anger

"When I'm angry, it's because I know I'm worth being angry about."

Anger is a natural response to abuse. As a child, you weren't allowed to express that anger. Instead, you may have turned it in on yourself, or maybe you lashed out at others. You may have hated and hurt yourself. You may even have stuffed down your anger with food, drugs, or alcohol. You may have even wanted to kill yourself. On the other hand, you may have become abusive, using your anger to control and intimidate others.

But anger doesn't have to hurt you or your loved ones. It can be a powerful energy that inspires you to change your life.

Fear of Anger

Many survivors are afraid of getting angry because their past experiences with anger were frightening or violent.

In your family you may have witnessed anger that was destructive and out of control. But there is a difference between violence and anger. Anger is a feeling, and feelings themselves do not hurt anyone.

When we feel angry, we have choices about how we express that anger. One man described how he is learning to make new choices:

> "I can instantly become Mr. Road Rage. Someone cuts me off on the highway and I act like they dropped a nuclear bomb on my hometown. I get enraged. I honk my horn, race to try to catch up so I can scream at them—all that ridiculous, self-destructive stuff.
>
> "But I do it a lot less often than I used to. Instead I go to the cheapest therapy—the batting cage. During times of stress I head down there once a week. I plunk in the quarters and they spit those softballs at you. I picture someone's face on that softball as I whack away at it. I can swing as hard as I want and not do any damage. After a half hour of that, I feel great."

As you welcome your anger and become familiar with it, you can direct it to meet your needs—like an experienced rider controlling a powerful horse.

Anger is a natural response to abuse.

"I'd Like to Kill Him"

At one point or another, many survivors have strong feelings of wanting to get back at the people who hurt them so terribly. Wanting revenge is a natural response to abuse. But don't act on your fantasies. If you meet violence with violence, you stoop to the level of your abuser. As one survivor said, "I've learned to respect human life more than he ever did."

There are many ways to express your anger positively and safely.

For some survivors, expressing anger physically is empowering. They have shredded newspapers or broken old dishes where no one could get hurt. Others have taken political action—organizing Take Back the Night marches or working to change laws that continue protecting abusers.

For some, clearly stating the facts is enough: "My coach took advantage of me. He robbed me of my childhood and I'm mad as hell about that!" Saying these words out loud to a sympathetic listener— or simply writing in your journal can be an effective way to express your anger.

Anger and Love

Anger and love are not incompatible. Most of us have been angry, at one time or another, with everyone we love.

Getting angry at your abuser doesn't have to wipe out the positive parts of your history. You can be furious about the abuse and still hold on to things from your childhood that nourished you.

Anger As a Part of Life

As you become more familiar with your anger, it stops being a dangerous monster and becomes one of many feelings you might have in a day. Anger can be so safe that even children aren't scared by it. One woman bought a giant stuffed frog for two dollars at a garage sale. Her whole family has benefited:

> "When one of us gets really angry, we stomp all over it.
> Even as a very small child, my daughter would explain,
> 'It's okay to beat up Big Frog because he's not alive. It

doesn't really hurt him.' At times when I was crabby she would tell me: 'Go get Big Frog, Mom. You can yell all you want. There's nobody here but me and you, and I don't mind.'"

The Benefits of Anger

Anger motivates us to take action and guides us toward positive change. It can also be the thing that moves us beyond despair. One woman recalled:

> "If I was to name one reason I got through it, it would be the anger. I kept saying to myself, 'Are you going to let him win out?' If for no other reason, I forced myself to get better. I was hell-bent on surviving, if only to show him that I was going to outlast him. My anger fueled me to get well. When I would be raging, my therapist would say to me, 'Hold on to that anger. That's your best friend.'"

Anger has inspired survivors to cut ties with abusers, to end abusive marriages, to quit jobs with hostile bosses, and to break addictions to drugs and alcohol. Focusing anger on the abuser—and away from yourself or your loved ones—clears the way for self-care and positive action in the world.

Anger motivates us to take action and guides us toward positive change.

Forgiveness?

"You don't sit around trying to forgive Hitler. There are a lot of better things to do with a life."

Many survivors try desperately to forgive the abuser. They despair that they can't heal without it. But it is *not* necessary to forgive the abuser in order to heal from child sexual abuse. The only person you have to forgive is *yourself*.

Eventually you will have to come to some sort of resolution in your feelings about the abuser so you can move on. Whether or not this resolution includes forgiveness is a personal matter:

> "I haven't worked at forgiveness because time is short and life is precious. I want to focus on exposing perpetrators and helping other survivors heal. If along the way forgiveness happens, that's great. If not, that's okay too."

"Oh, Honey, Just Forgive and Forget"

It is never helpful to tell survivors that they need to forgive the people who abused them. Yet it's likely that you will be given this advice by people who don't want to see you suffer or who are uncomfortable with your grief or anger.

If you have strong religious beliefs, you may feel it is your duty to forgive. Or you may fear that you can't heal if you don't forgive. But forgiving your abuser or the members of your family who didn't protect you is *not* a required part of the healing process.

When you begin to heal, it's important to focus on what happened to you and what it has meant in your life. *Trying* to forgive can get in the way of doing this necessary work.

Forgiveness is a very personal matter. It may not be part of your journey, but if it is, it will happen only when you've fully experienced the grief, the anger, and the other stages of healing. Forgiveness is a by-product of the process, not the final reward.

It is *not* necessary to forgive the abuser in order to
heal from child sexual abuse.

But They Had a Bad Childhood

Laura remembers her mother coming home from her job as a social worker and telling stories about the people she worked with:

> "She'd take us to Burger Chef, and over the french fries she'd tell us about a sixteen-year-old murderer or a fifteen-year-old rapist. We'd look up from our Cokes and ask, 'But why, Mom? Why would anyone do something like that?' Her answer was always the same. She'd pick up her double hamburger and say, 'They had a bad childhood.'"

It's true that many abusers were abused as children, but that doesn't justify their behavior. The vast majority of survivors do not go on to abuse children. Regardless of childhood pain, there is no excuse for sexual abuse. As one survivor put it:

> "I would never in a million years forgive my father. He had a choice. He made a choice. I've had choices in my life that were just as difficult. Sometimes I've failed. But for the most part I try very hard not to. And I don't think he tried one bit. I think he gave in to his impulses every time."

You May Feel Compassion

As you move through the healing process, you may find yourself feeling compassion for those who have hurt you or failed to protect you:

> "There's a picture in my mind of my mother standing in the hallway with all of us kids. My father was in the bathroom beating my brother. We're crying, 'Daddy! Daddy!' And my mother's saying, 'Don, don't! Oh, Don, don't!' And she's right there crying with us. She was as much a part of the helplessness as we were. I really believe she did the best she could do. It wasn't very good, but it was the best she could do."

When survivors come naturally to a place of compassion or forgiveness, it can bring a new sense of freedom. One woman explained:

> "The intensity in my feelings is gone since I've forgiven him. I don't wake up feeling like if I had his picture, I'd

throw daggers at it. I can say, 'Your face no longer scares me. Your name no longer puts me in fear.'"

Forgiveness can release us from the hold the abuser once had on us and open new doors in our healing:

"Finding forgiveness toward my abuser has been an important part of my healing. It enabled me to soften my heart toward myself."

Forgiving Yourself

The only person you must forgive is yourself. If you are still blaming yourself or feeling ashamed of the things you've done to cope, you will have to forgive yourself. You will have to stop blaming the child who was vulnerable, the child who felt pleasure, the child who survived the best he or she could.

The only person you must forgive is yourself.

You must forgive yourself for not knowing how to protect yourself. You must forgive yourself for needing the time to heal now. And you must give yourself all the kindness and compassion you can, so you can direct your attention and energy toward your own healing. *This* forgiveness is what's important.

Spirituality

"There was a voice inside me that said, 'You'll get there.' I took hope and courage from that voice. It was my spirituality."

Spirituality can bring great comfort when you are healing from child sexual abuse. Whether you trust in God, belong to a religious community, or follow your own personal path, connecting to a power greater than yourself can sustain you when everything seems to be falling apart:

> "When all else failed, I would hold on to the things I knew were true. The sun rose every morning. It set every night. People since the beginning of time have suffered great losses and pain. Yet they went on.
>
> "We don't get to choose what happens to us, only how we respond to it. I'd think about the kind of person I wanted to be, that I wanted to keep my heart open, even though it hurt so much. That I wanted to be kind. I'd hold on to these deeper truths and I prayed that they'd be a raft that could carry me through the pain."

Believing in God or praying in community can be deeply healing. Yet many survivors have lost their faith. They feel that God didn't protect them. One woman explained:

> "I was in a very conservative religious group for twenty years. I thought Jesus could heal me. When I started having memories of sexual abuse, the first thing I thought was, 'What kind of God have I been believing in?' A little girl had been beaten and raped and no God did anything about it."

If the abuse was perpetrated by a religious leader, your beliefs may have been shattered. One survivor of abuse by a priest explained:

> "Trust and faith were broken for me in a very profound way because the church *was* my life as a child. I still can't set foot in a church without feeling traumatized.
>
> "I've come to realize that spirituality is not about where you worship on Sundays. It's how you feel about yourself and what you do with your life.
>
> "When I speak out about my abuse and reach other victims, it raises my spirit higher and higher. Being able to speak out publicly is an answer to my prayers. I've found my own version of spirituality and it's not in brick and mortar."

"I've had to find my own version of spirituality and it's not in brick and mortar."

Becoming Whole

A universal part of spirituality is feeling connected to life around you. You experience this in nature as you watch waves roll in, look out over vast prairies, or walk in the desert. You touch this special place when you hold a new baby, listen to inspiring music, or share deeply with someone you love. It's the miracle of life.

When you see cocoons turn into butterflies, it's a little easier to believe that a damaged human being can become whole—even if that human being is you. Spirituality means staying in touch with the part of you that is choosing to heal, that wants to be healthy and fully alive.

> When you can see cocoons turn into
> butterflies, it's a little easier to believe that a
> damaged human being can become whole—
> even if that human being is you.

The person you want to become is already inside you. Getting in touch with the stillness within can help you see that you are more than just a person in pain.

Finding Faith

Survivors often obsess about healing. There may be periods when you think of little else. Some of this is natural and unavoidable. But beyond a certain point, it can hinder you.

Often we obsess about our abuse because we don't believe the healing process is really working. We think we have to try hard every minute or we'll lose ground. This isn't true. We often make our greatest strides when we give ourselves time and space to absorb the healing work we've already done.

As you relax and trust your ability to heal yourself, you gain confidence that you will make it. You start to believe in yourself.

Spirituality can be a source of inspiration, courage, and love.

Believing in something more constant than your own shifting emotions can be a great comfort as you heal. Spirituality can be a source of inspiration, courage, and love.

The Process of Change

"My grandfather was dead and gone and I was alive with the same problems I'd always had. I had to face the fact that if I wanted a different life, I was going to have to do something about it."

When you first start dealing with your abuse, you may be relieved finally to have someone to blame for your problems. There is a reason for your suffering. You were sexually abused.

But eventually, you realize things aren't that simple or fair. It's not enough to know you were abused. You also have to change your life. One survivor explained:

> "I had to go from dealing with the incest an hour a week in therapy to dealing with it in my real life. I *changed* my relationship. I *changed* my job. I *changed* my home. I started getting angry. I started to cry. I've really changed. I *look* different. I *sound* different. I *changed* my life."

It's not enough to know you were abused. You also have to change your life.

How to Change

- **Become aware of the behavior you want to change.** Is there something you're doing that isn't good for you? Are you staying in a bad relationship? Are you drinking too much? Are you blowing up at the people you love? Are you helping everyone except yourself?
- **Look at the reasons you developed that behavior in the first place.** When did you first feel or act that way? Why?
- **Have compassion for what you've done in the past.** Even if you didn't make the best choices, you did the best you could at the time. And now you can make better choices. Focus on that.
- **Find new ways to meet your needs.** When you learn to fulfill your needs in new ways, it will be easier to let go of your old behavior.
- **Get support.** The people around you affect your ability to change. People who are working to grow in their lives will support your efforts to change.
- **Name your fears.** It's scary to change. We usually give up something in order to make room for something new. Looking at why you're scared can lessen the power of your fears.
- **Fear doesn't have to stop you.** Everyone feels scared when they change, even if it's a change for the better. If you're scared, you can act anyway.
- **Old habits don't change easily.** When you try to change an old habit, it sometimes seems to get worse. Don't give up at this critical point. The "I can't stand it anymore" feeling often means you're close to the change you've been wanting to make.
- **Make several tries.** Making changes is usually a slow, trial-and-error process. Yet each little step forward leads to real change and a better life.

- **Keep trying.** Don't give up. Most of the changes we make in life require repetition. If not smoking *one* cigarette were enough, it wouldn't be so hard to quit smoking.
- **Be gentle with yourself.** Be patient. Forgive yourself when you go back to an old behavior you're trying to change. Don't punish yourself.
- **Give yourself credit.** Take time to feel proud of yourself when you have a success. Don't just run to the next mountain.
- **Celebrate.** Treat yourself well when you have a victory.

Resolution and Moving On

"I feel like I'm home-free. I still have a lot of work to do, but I know it can be done. I know what the tools are and I know how to use them. When I talk about the incest now, a lot of it is about the healing and the success and the joy."

At the beginning of the healing process, it can be hard to imagine that you will ever stop suffering. It may seem like the rest of your life will be overshadowed by sexual abuse. But if you make the commitment to heal and follow through, you will eventually reach a place of resolution and peace.

Jean Williams is an incest survivor and the child of an alcoholic parent. After many years of healing, she had an experience that dramatically changed her point of view:

"I went to Mexico for a few months and I really learned a lot by living in another culture. When I came back my mail was full of flyers about self-improvement programs. And I thought, *My God! I don't want to improve myself anymore. I'm good enough the way I am!*"

Moving on can't be forced or rushed. Yet from the moment you begin to deal with the abuse, people will urge you to hurry up and "put it in the past." There will be times you want to move on as well—simply because healing is so painful. But moving on to avoid the pain or to please others is an escape.

Real moving on is the natural result of fully living through each step of the healing process.

Feeling More Stable

Resolution comes when your feelings and point of view become steadier. The emotional roller coaster evens out. One man described it like this:

> "I no longer have nightmares. I've kept a job for five years without having major fights with my boss. It's been ten years since I was too scared to leave the house. I've stopped biting my fingernails till they bled. It's the absence of symptoms that makes me realize how far I've come.
>
> "The image that comes to mind is an old-fashioned pinball machine where the ball comes down and bounces against all these brightly colored things. That's how I lived my life for many years. I was at the mercy of uncontrollable feelings. I know now that no matter what life sends my way, nothing will crush me. I've already been through the worst, and that makes me free."

When you're in the early stages of the healing process, it can be hard to imagine that you'll ever stop suffering, but you will:

"Ten years ago, I never could have predicted that I would be this happy. Never. If I were talking to someone at the very beginning of this process, I'd say, 'It absolutely can and does get better. It's a long, long road. It's much more uphill than downhill, but you will get better.'"

Letting Go of the Damage

There may be times in the healing process when you lose touch with the fact that you're working so hard *in order to move on to something else in life.* Being a survivor is painful, but it can also bring you a sense of identity and pride that can be hard to give up:

"A lot of people get stuck in the rage and hatred and fear. But I realized I didn't have to hang on to it. I stopped sitting there picking open wounds, saying, 'If only I pick deep enough, I can see some real blood and gore.' I wanted to feel safe in the world.

"There was a point where I simply stopped carrying the bags. Every now and then the porter brings it to me and says, 'Here's your baggage, ma'am.' And I open it up and go through it again. Then I say, 'I've seen enough of you for now. I want to go on with my life again.' And life feels much better. It's a tremendous relief to stop suffering all the time."

As you put the abuse in perspective, it becomes one part of your history, not your whole life:

"You can look at my life and say there've been some real tragedies, and there have been. But there've also been some exquisitely beautiful times. To me, those far outweigh the others."

Letting Go of Crisis

It's easy to get used to intensity and drama, but being in constant crisis keeps you from moving on. It's a major milestone when you stop generating one crisis after another. Yet you're likely to feel empty and uncertain when there's no emergency to cope with. Wait it out. The rewards are worth it.

When you learn to balance life's challenges with quiet, peaceful times, you make room to enjoy the smaller, daily pleasures. Cooking dinner, reading, dancing, talking to a friend, playing basketball, growing flowers, and listening to music can all be deeply satisfying.

> Part of healing is doing the things you've always
> wanted to do. You don't have to wait until you're
> "completely healed" to begin enjoying your
> present life.

Healing is not about endless struggle. Part of healing is doing the things you've always wanted to do. You don't have to wait until you're "completely healed" to begin enjoying your present life.

And it's only when you're not in crisis that you can work toward some of your dreams.

Resolving Relationships

Part of moving on is coming to terms with the people who abused you, didn't protect you, or don't support you now. You get a clear idea of how you feel about each of them and you decide what, if any, relationship you want with them in the future.

Survivors often waste precious energy hoping to get people in their lives to change, apologize, or take responsibility. When this happens, it can lead to powerful healing. But often these wishes are fantasies. It's important to evaluate each relationship thoughtfully and to base your decisions on what is realistic.

When the truth is fully acknowledged and sincere apologies are made, deep healing can take place. When this isn't possible, you may still choose to accept a limited relationship because aspects of it are worthwhile to you. Other times, you may decide that further contact is neither possible nor desirable. In that case, you will have to make peace inside yourself with the relationship.

When you reach a place of resolution with your family or the abuser, the effect is often dramatic. When you stop hoping for the impossible, you open the doors for real help and support.

Becoming Whole

As you heal, you see yourself more realistically. You accept that you are a person with strengths and weaknesses. You make the changes you can in your life and let go of things that aren't in your power to change.

You learn that every part of you is valuable. And you realize that all of your thoughts and feelings are important, even when they're painful or difficult:

"I thought when you were healed, everything felt good, but it isn't true. I wanted to select certain things—humor, warmth, love, fun. I didn't want to feel scared or angry or any 'negative feelings.' But they're all part of being human."

Every part of you is valuable and important.

There Is No End of the Line

There is no finish line to healing. You can't erase your history. The abuse affected you deeply. That will never change. But you can come to a place of peace, gradually accepting that the healing process will continue throughout your life:

"Finally, I had to realize it was part of me. It's not something I can get rid of. The way I work with it will change, but it will always be there. If I'm going to love myself totally, then I have to love all of me, and this is part of who I am."

Most survivors make the decision to heal from a place of pain, shame, and fear. At the beginning, the work feels like a burden. But eventually, you realize that healing has brought you more than just the lessening of pain. You start to see the healing process as the beginning of a lifetime of growth. As one survivor put it, "I have no intention of stopping. I fully intend to grow until I die."

At the beginning, the work feels like a burden. But eventually, you see the healing process as the beginning of a lifetime of growth.

Part Two

Stories of Courage

I Told My Son: Eva's Story

Eva Smith is an African American in her early thirties who lives in California.* She is a therapist and an artist. She lives with her two teenage children. "I share this information as a gift of healing for other women. I am truly living my life now, after just surviving for so many years."

Between the ages of three and eight, I was molested by my great-uncle. From nine to fifteen, my stepfather molested me. I grew up just trying to live from day to day and survive. I used to pray my stepfather would get struck by lightning. I wasn't above making a pact with the devil to get rid of him. *Anything.* And anything happened. I got pregnant.

I had always been a fat child. When I was thirteen, I weighed 188 pounds. And then I lost weight. So when I got pregnant, everybody just thought I was getting fat again. I'll never forget—I was going into my junior year in high school and my mother and I went shopping for clothes. She came into the dressing room, looked

* Eva Smith chose to use a pseudonym.

at me, and said, "You look different." And I said, "I'm just getting fat again." And she said, "I'm taking you to the doctor." That was in September, and considering that my son was born in November, I must have been at least seven months pregnant, but all this was brand-new to me.

When the doctor told my mother I was pregnant, she asked me who the father was, and I told her. She confronted my stepfather and he claimed that he knew nothing about it. Within a week, we left him and went down South.

When I first realized I was pregnant, I attempted suicide. It was a hard time for me. *I* knew I needed therapy. I wish somebody else realized it at the time!

My mother told me I didn't have to keep the child. She said I could put it up for adoption or that she would raise it as her own. I chose to keep that child because it was the first thing that was ever mine.

I created a cover story about who the father was. I said he was some boy I'd been going with. I had to deal with a lot of put-downs from people 'cause I was fifteen and having this baby.

Because of all the things that happened to me, there was this question that used to haunt me: "Why me?" Those were the years I call my trauma years. And I went from my trauma years into being a battered wife.

He Had the License

I got married at seventeen. I was already pregnant with my daughter. We were already into it before we ever got married. We used to argue once a week when we were going together, but not real physical stuff. But after we were married, he had the license. You know, they pronounce you man and *wife*, not man and *woman.* To my way of thinking it gives men a free ticket to do whatever they want. So the battering started and increased till I couldn't take it.

I was making $1.79 an hour. I was paying all the bills. I was buying all the food, the clothes, even renting him a television. I got off work at 4:30. I was supposed to catch the bus at 4:35, hit downtown at 5:00, change buses, and walk in the door at 5:20. If I walked in the door at 5:30, I got my ass kicked.

So in essence, he held my children hostage. He did lots of sadistic things to me. My nerves were so bad I was going through temporary blindness. I was on a large dose of Librium.

I was twenty then, and I tried to kill myself. I had gotten my prescription filled. I came home and took half the bottle. He found the bottle and woke me up 'cause I was going off to la-la land. And he got me up and went and got my son, who was four at the time. He sprayed Raid in his hair; then he took a lighter and held it over his head and said, "If you don't wake up, I'm gonna light his hair." I mean I was going through it. We didn't have a phone or anything. There's that isolation thing.

I decided to kill him. I knew we couldn't live together without one of us killing the other. So I was going to kill him. I planned that Friday when I got paid, I'd pay the rent, the water bill, buy a gun, go home, walk in the door, scream, and kill him. Even now, I can say with conviction I was going to kill him.

And this woman who was like my second mother said, "You don't want that on your head for the rest of your life." So I turned him over to the military 'cause he'd gone AWOL. They took him to jail. I took the children to safety and moved out in four days. I started divorce proceedings immediately.

When I got rid of my husband, all that weird stuff went away. The blindness and the shaking went away. I didn't have to take Librium.

So by the time I was twenty-one, I had been married, divorced, and had two children. When I moved to California, I had seven suitcases, two kids, and one hundred dollars. And Lord, I've come a long way from there.

I Have Told My Son

My son will be eighteen this fall, and when he was thirteen, I told him who his father was. He had been asking questions on a regular basis. When he was younger, I told him my cover story—that his father was a teenager I had sex with. That was okay then, but as he got older, when he'd ask questions about his father, there'd be a hush in the room or people would change the subject. So he got the feeling there was this secret. A number of people were in on this secret, and he wasn't one of them. There's no father on his birth certificate, so there was always this air of mystery. And at thirteen he just asked me in a more straightforward way than he ever had before, so I decided to tell him.

Ahmal—the man I was involved with at the time, who was a father figure for my children—and I got together and discussed it thoroughly. And then the three of us went into the bedroom. My son was trying to be grown-up, wanting to have a cigarette. Everybody was cool, you know. I think it's important to say how I told it to him because I didn't make it a real heavy-duty kind of thing.

I'm a storyteller, and I just told it like you'd tell any kind of story to a child. I had parts in it that made him laugh. I told it in a way that wasn't condemning my stepfather, because no matter how much pain he brought into my life, this man was my son's biological father, and whatever I told him was going to mold a certain part of him for the rest of his life. So it was important to me not to make my stepfather an ogre, to tell my son about it in such a way that he would not be as devastated as I was by it. Your children are more important than anything that may hurt you or the hate that you feel.

And so I dredged up every good memory about my stepfather that I could find. I worked at making him very human. I talked about his shortcomings and the good things about him. I talked about his smile, 'cause he had a wonderful smile. I didn't go into the sexual abuse real heavy because that was not the important thing at that point. I talked about what he did to me and how young I was. I put in a little drama, 'cause there was plenty of that, but I didn't make it a great big thing. And I talked about what it was like being pregnant with him. How I felt. I was fifteen. How that felt.

My son's first reaction was, "Wow, all of that happened to me!" And Ahmal said, "Hey, blood, check this out. None of that happened to you. It happened to your mother." And so my son had to deal with that. He had to weigh how this affected who he was as a person. It was a very difficult time for him. And it was a very, very hard time for me because he was trying to punish me for who his father was.

Slowly it has healed for my son. Now it's just a fact of being. I don't think he resents me for it. If anything, maybe he loves me a little more. He was a spirit that had to come here and that was the way he came.

It Had Happened to Me: Paul's Story

Paul Coffey is the oldest of two children born into a white middle-class family.* His childhood was secure and loving until he was five. Then his parents got divorced and his whole world changed. From then on there was very little stability in his life.

Paul is a thirty-eight-year-old teacher who lives in a small town in California.

When I was six, the kids in my neighborhood discovered a hidden box of pornographic magazines under a house. They showed people doing all kinds of crazy stuff. Every kid on the block got invited over to see it. It was powerful material. The magazines were intriguing and graphic and repulsive all at the same time. Our reactions were, "What is that?," "Oh my God!," and "Gross!" A lot of us got into body exploration with each other because of what we'd seen.

Right about then I had a sleepover with a friend. We were

---

* Paul Coffey chose to use a pseudonym.

camped out in his backyard and we were doing some innocent sex play. Then his teenage cousin came into the tent and took over. The "games" became more and more intense and I didn't like them at all. My last memory is of being turned over and pushed down on my stomach, and feeling this terrible pain in my butt. I don't remember what happened after that.

That experience was traumatic and freaky. It was scary and I didn't understand what had happened. I remember thinking, "This is a strange, terrible thing I brought on myself." I was sure it was my fault because my friend and I had been doing sex play.

Like most children, I never told anybody. I never cried or showed any distress. I just tucked it away as if it had never happened. It was an early experience of something going really wrong really fast without me being able to do anything about it.

He Was Nasty, but He Was Smart About It

When I was eleven, we moved in with my mother's boyfriend, Frank. He was bad news and my sister and I could smell it immediately. He was nasty, but he was smart about it. He never did anything in front of the wrong people.

Frank was a big man. He was six feet four inches and 220 pounds. He had a black belt in karate and he was a psychologist. He was sharp and he had no conscience. He was much nicer to his dog than he ever was to us.

Frank hurt me physically a lot. He'd get me in a choke hold and show me how easy it would be for him to kill me. He'd hold me like that until I passed out.

Other times, he'd come into my room when I was alone and close the door behind him. He'd ask if I was masturbating and how it felt. He was very invasive, though he never touched me sexually.

He did sexually abuse my sister though. She didn't tell anyone for a long time. Finally, when she was thirteen, she told my mother. As soon as my mother found out, she kicked Frank out. But for years my mother had missed the fact that the incest was happening right under her nose.

I Never Said a Word About It to Anyone

When I was thirteen, I went to live with my father. Shortly afterward, my dad was directing a commercial. I was with him on the shoot and I had to go to the bathroom. One of the guys on the set followed me and closed the door. I was terrified.

I was standing at the urinal. This man came up behind me and said, "You're very beautiful. I love those pants. What are they made out of?" Then he put his hands on them. He started touching me and saying what a nice body I had. I didn't say anything, but inside I was freaking out.

Just like in the tent, there was something exciting and compelling about what was going on. I was drawn to it and repulsed by it at the same time. Finally I ran out of the bathroom before anything else could happen. I never said a word to anyone.

The incident in the bathroom happened just as I was entering puberty. I was overwhelmed by the sexual awakening in my body. All this sexual energy was running through me and I had weird ideas about what to do with it. From my experience in the tent, I learned that sexual desires were something you forced on someone. At the same time, I knew how horrible that could be. I felt conflicted about the whole thing.

When I was at my mom's house, I shared a bed with my sister. I started initiating sexual games with her. We'd lie next to each other and touch each other's private parts. We'd ask each other permis-

sion. Sometimes she'd say yes. Sometimes she'd say no. Things esca-
lated from there. I was always the one who pushed our explorations
further than she wanted them to go.

It Had Happened to Me

When I was twenty-three I began to recognize the trauma I'd suffered as a boy. I had never forgotten what happened in the tent. I
remembered everything up until the point I blacked out, but I had
always thought it happened to some other little boy.

One night I was driving in L.A., listening to the radio, when I
suddenly realized that that boy had been me. Yet, like many men, I
denied that I had been hurt or that I needed help.

It was my mother who insisted I go to therapy. She told me, "We
all need help with things in our lives. There's nothing wrong with
talking to someone."

I said, "I don't need help! I'm smart. I'm creative. I don't have a
problem! You don't know what's best for me!"

My mother replied, "Don't you think it's difficult to say something is no good until you've tried it? Why don't you just try therapy? I'll pay for it."

I really couldn't argue with that, so I took her up on it.

I Was Able to Admit I Needed Help

Once I got into therapy, I was able to admit that I was having trouble in certain parts of my life. I was so shy I couldn't even ask a girl
out. I was not comfortable with myself sexually. I started to realize
that maybe I did have some things to work on.

Still, I worried that my friends would laugh at me, that they'd see me as weak or weird. Growing up, I'd learned that a good man is strong, can figure things out for himself, and doesn't need help. Men aren't supposed to have feelings or be vulnerable. So for me to say, "I'm hurt and I need help," was like saying, "Maybe I'm not really a man."

But the pain I was in was like water building up behind a dam. The pressure kept building until I could no longer deny that I had been hurt. Finally my desire to heal became stronger than my fear. I was able to admit I needed help.

Once I decided to do the work, the floodgates opened. I felt dizzy and overwhelmed having to face all the feelings I had stuffed during my childhood: my fears, my shame, my confusion, my anger. I had to get real about the things I did and the things that were done to me.

In the beginning, therapy was hard for me. Men are supposed to focus on their achievements, not sit in a room talking about themselves. But I had made a commitment to heal and healing takes time. I needed time to go to therapy. I needed downtime afterward. I had to learn to focus on my feelings instead of on the tasks I thought I should be accomplishing.

It's Been Fifteen Years Since I Started to Heal

At times the work has been intense, but my life is awesome right now. I feel completely different in my body than I did when I was twenty. I no longer feel like something terrible is about to happen. For years, I'd be eating breakfast or walking down the street, terrified, thinking, *What kind of doom is going to fall on me next?* I was sure that every situation could turn bad at any minute. Now I see the universe as a benign place. I have a sense of power in the world.

My sister and I are very close. In the last ten years we've spent many hours talking about what we experienced. We realized that we both had been hurt.

We've talked about our anger and about forgiveness. We've come back to really loving each other and being there for each other.

I've learned that being a man isn't much different from being a woman. It's just being human. It's being honest and loving and willing. It's being caring and passionate and connected.

I'm engaged to be married and I'm experiencing that kind of love for the first time. Intimacy is something I never thought I'd be able to have.

I have a sense of peace I never had before. And I wouldn't have had any of that if I hadn't made the commitment to heal.

Learning to Survive: Soledad's Story

Soledad is a twenty-eight-year-old Chicana who was severely abused by her father throughout her childhood.* Today she is a high school counselor in Sonoma County, California.

Soledad writes, "In this interview, I have spoken more of my biological parents (due to my feelings of betrayal and violation) than of my Tias and Tio, who were very much my parents, in the true sense of the word. Without them, I am convinced I would not have survived. I am certain my life would have been beaten or suffocated out of me. To them I owe my life. And because of them, I will struggle to keep it.

"I once read that we can give two things to children—one is a sense of roots and the other is a sense of wings. I now know my roots, my history. Now I am ready to fly toward the sun."

---

* Soledad chose to use a pseudonym.

Being Latina is real precious to me. However, part of the culture I hate is the silence. As beautiful as our language is, we don't have words for this. Our history is passed orally, yet there's such silence in Latino families about this.

There was no talk about sex in the house ever. It was all out on the streets. And how can you go to a woman you haven't been able to talk to about your damn period and tell her that her husband is raping you?

I think this kind of silence might be common, but it's especially true because my people feel so powerless in this culture, fearing authorities outside the family. We had to stick together and protect each other from the system, and the white people who control it. What other options did we have? We just had to keep it in. Admitting any problem would reflect badly on our whole culture.

And that's why it's hard for me to talk about it. I don't want anyone to use this against people of color, because there are so many negative stereotypes of Latinos already. And I don't want to promote more distrust of men of color. But this is how it happened for me and I need to break the silence.

My Father Was Like a Volcanic Eruption

I was raised in an extended family in Los Angeles in a hard-core ghetto. I'm the oldest of three kids. My dad worked on and off in factories. My mom worked in sweatshops. We not only lived in poverty, we *were* poverty.

I was beaten at least every other day for years. I hated that my parents beat us, but everybody around us got whipped, so that was just the way it was. At least when my mother beat us, we still had a feeling she loved us. It hurt less.

My father was like a volcanic eruption. You wouldn't know

when it was going to happen, but when it did, there was no stopping it. He wore these steel-toed shoes for work, and he'd kick us everywhere, including the head. You could get arrested for kicking a dog like that.

My father not only molested me, he molested all my cousins and all the girls in the neighborhood. The ones that I know, there are at least twenty-four. People trusted him with their kids. He was a great social manipulator. He knew how kids thought. It's amazing how one person can mess with so many kids.

From what I can tell, the sexual abuse started right when I was brought home from the hospital. In the beginning there was a lot of fondling. He could be what you would call "gentle," but I would interpret that as being sneaky, because I knew he could kill me. If you know that this man can kill you so easily, you're not going to say anything. And so I would just be frozen, with the feeling, "Soon it will be over." But it got worse and worse.

The peak of it all was at about eight. That's when he first raped me. It was pretty regular after that, at least three times a week. It happened in a lot of different places. We lived in really small quarters with no privacy. So he'd tell me we had to go out for milk, or that we needed to go for a ride in the car. He loved to take all the girls out for a ride. Most of this stuff happened in the car, a lot of it in the dark, so this left a blank for me because a lot of it I didn't see.

A lot of the raping happened from behind. When he abused me, he would talk to me in Spanish, threatening to cut my throat or cut my tongue out. So now, telling you my story in English is easier. I would probably be sobbing by now if I was describing in Spanish what he had done.

When I was thirteen the sexual abuse stopped. I had gotten more streetwise than ever, and he started to be fearful of me. He knew I was ready to die, and that I would fight him to our graves if I had to.

I Lived on the Streets

I was very self-destructive. I started taking drugs at nine. I started hustling. I did drugs and wouldn't even know what the hell I was taking. I didn't care.

Fighting was an everyday thing on the streets. As we got bigger, the toys got more dangerous. I carried knives. I got into fights with people who carried knives. And some with guns. You never knew if you'd come out alive.

Between what was happening at home and having to fight on the streets, I always thought the only freedom would be to go to prison. Then I would be free.

I dealt with my life hour by hour. For a long time, I never did want to live. I'd be five and I'd think, "Maybe I won't live until I'm ten," and I would hope that would be true. Or I'd get to be ten, and I'd think, "Okay, fifteen, max. That's as long as I'm going to live."

What other choices did I have? I grew up poor. Life was just the way it was. I never knew there was a way out.

There Was More to Life Than What I Knew

I was always in and out of school. I was illiterate. But a teacher took an interest in me when I was sixteen. She cared about me and thought I had a good mind. She was scared of me but wanted to find out why I was the way I was. She started talking to me and spending time with me. It mattered to her that I didn't destroy myself. And that made all the difference. There wasn't anyone before who had ever spent that kind of time with me.

Learning to read helped me see that there was more to life than what I knew. That was the beginning of my healing. It was the first time I thought that maybe I could survive without hustling. Maybe

I could learn something from some book and get some power from it. Get some options.

I was lucky. I got into an Upward Bound program. The teacher helped me get into college. It was a real culture shock. I hadn't ever been around that many white people. I still couldn't read enough to understand the menus in the cafeteria. But I stuck it out.

I Was Barely Keeping Myself Alive

Even though I succeeded in going to school and getting a job, I knew things weren't right inside. For a long time all I did was come home and lay on my bed. Sometimes I'd turn the TV on. My dinner would be a Coke. Maybe I'd decide to have a real dinner, and I'd have a pint of ice cream. That was my life. I'd never open the drapes, answer the phone, or open the door. I was barely keeping myself alive.

About a year and a half ago, my cousin called me up and said, "Did you know that your dad molested my sisters?"

I said, "I never really thought about him that way. But it doesn't surprise me."

I went over to visit her and we stayed up the whole night and the whole day to talk about it. It was painful, but I felt vindicated. I knew I wasn't crazy. There were reasons I was destroying myself. I finally knew why I hated him so much. I had always thought people were born hating their fathers.

From then on, I couldn't stop thinking about it. I was obsessed. And I started to understand all these things. I started to wake up feeling powerful. I'd always had to carry a knife or be hustling to feel powerful before. All of a sudden I had a belief in myself.

I Never Had Plants Before

I feel lighter, like a real burden has come off me. If I had run away from the pain, I think I would still be destroying myself in some way.

It's a small thing, but I never had plants before. It's my way of trying to keep something other than me alive. It gives me a lot of pleasure. I grew up where there weren't too many flowers, right in the middle of the damn city.

I got my first plant about six months ago. Now I have all sorts of flowers on my porch. I have big bushes with purple flowers. I have big round pots with different flowers in them. I wanted color around me. It's real Latina, all these colors. It reminds me a lot of my aunts.

It's a reason to live, really. I was scared about it at first. But now I know I can nurture them and keep them healthy. After I've been so rough in my life, I can still take care of something so delicate.

Taking On the Church:
David's Story

David Clohessy is the second of six children from a very traditional Catholic home.* They lived two blocks from the church. He had an aunt who was a nun and his brother went on to become a priest. David attended parochial schools and his parents were very involved in the church.

David describes how he was molested between the ages of twelve and sixteen by Father John Whiteley in the Diocese of Jefferson City, and repressed all memories of the events until he was in his early thirties.

David went on to volunteer for a decade as the director of the nation's largest support group for clergy sexual abuse victims, the Survivors Network of those Abused by Priests (SNAP). In 2002, he became the organization's first paid staff person.†

---

* David Clohessy is using his real name.
† SNAP supports both men and women who were abused by clergy

When I was eleven, we got a new priest, Father John Whiteley. He went to great pains to ingratiate himself into our family. He complimented my parents. He came over for dinner. He hung around on the weekends. At that time, it was the dream of all Catholic parents to have a priest take an interest in their children. There was nothing the least bit suspicious about it. It was a cause for joy, rather than alarm.

Father Whiteley had a mailing to do for the church and he asked if I'd come to the rectory to help stuff envelopes. Afterward, he gave me a ride home and said, "I'm going to repay you for your help. I'm going to take you out to dinner sometime."

He called several days later to invite me out to eat. It was a big deal. We weren't a rich family and we had six kids, so we didn't go out to dinner very often. I was thrilled. I got into Father Whiteley's car and he said, "Where would you like to go?" That startled me. No one had ever asked me where I wanted to go before.

It was like being in a fairy tale. Here was this priest who seemed wonderful and charming and interested in me. My parents respected him and he wanted to spend time with me. We had wonderful conversations. It was so flattering to have a grown-up take me seriously and ask my opinion.

Over time, Father Whiteley started taking me on weekend canoeing and camping trips. The first time I ever saw the ocean was with this guy. The first time I ever saw the mountains was with this guy. The first time I ever went to New Orleans was with this guy.

The first time he abused me we were down at the Lake of the

---

members. If you'd like more information or would like to talk to someone who understands, call SNAP at 312-409-2720. Or visit the SNAP Web site (www.survivorsnetwork.org) for a wealth of articles, resources, and support groups.

Ozarks. It was a summer night and we were sleeping in the back of his van. We were lying on top of the sleeping bags in the back. I had a stomach ache and he offered to put his hand on my stomach. It seemed odd, but I said okay. We lay there for a long time and gradually he kept moving his hand down until he was touching my penis.

I froze. I thought he must be asleep, but then he fondled me. I was petrified. I didn't say anything and neither did he.

By the next morning, I had forgotten all about it. It was like nothing had ever happened. And that pattern continued for all the years he abused me. He always abused me when we were out of town, alone, late at night, either as I was about to go to sleep or when I was asleep. Nothing was ever said. I'd wake up in the morning as if nothing had happened. I'd come home and tell my parents what a great time we had. And I wasn't lying. I literally had no recall whatsoever.

This continued until I was sixteen. We went on eight or twelve trips a year. The pattern was the same, and I never remembered any of the abuse.

I Had a Problem in Those Days

Fast-forward fifteen years. I was thiry-one years old. I went to the movies with Laura, the woman who is now my wife. We saw *Nuts*, with Barbra Streisand. Now I'm not the kind of person who gets all worked up, but I got extremely upset watching that film, and I didn't know why. Adrenaline started flowing through me and I could barely sit in my seat. I really wanted to "get" the bad guy, who was a perpetrator.

If you had asked me, walking into the movie, "Have you ever been sexually abused or do you know anyone who has been?" I would have said, "Absolutely not." And if I had walked into that movie and seen Father John Whiteley, I'd have gone up to him and given him a big hug, like I would an old friend.

After the movie, Laura and I went out to eat. I was so agitated I couldn't concentrate on what she was saying to me. I kept flashing back to scenes in the movie. Later, when we went to bed, I tossed and turned and couldn't calm down. At two in the morning, I had my first memory—of the time he molested me at the Lake of the Ozarks.

I started crying and I squeezed Laura real tight and said, "What happened to that little girl in the movie happened to me."

She listened, but didn't push me to say more.

Soon after, I wrote to Father John and said, "I remember what you did and I never want to see you again."

He immediately called and said he wanted to talk. He was very persistent. Finally, we met at a restaurant. Father John never denied abusing me. He acknowledged that he had done things he shouldn't have done. He said he knew he "had a problem back in those years," but that he had "taken care of his problem." He talked about going away to a couple of treatment centers.

We talked for fifteen minutes. I kept feeling more and more uncomfortable. Finally, I asked him, "I just have to know this. Did you abuse any of my siblings?"

He said, "I really can't answer that because I don't want to violate anyone's privacy."

At that point, I got up and stormed out.

Eight Years of Healing

Knowing I was going to marry Laura, I thought that maybe I should deal with the abuse. So I decided to go to therapy. I walked into the therapist's office and said, "I'm here because I was molested by a priest for four years when I was a kid and I want to find out if it's had any impact on my life." Fortunately, the therapist didn't laugh.

I was in therapy on and off for the next eight years. During that time, I remembered more and more of what had happened to me.

A year into therapy, I told my parents. I was scared to death because we're not a family that talks about personal things. I drove eight hours to see them, but if they didn't react well, I was prepared to turn right around and drive back.

I couldn't bring myself to tell them the first day. But the second day, I said, "When I was a kid, Father John molested me." The minute I said that, my mother's face turned gray. Being the caregiver that I am, I started backpedaling immediately. "Well, it happened a long time ago. I've been in a lot of therapy. I'm okay now. It's not a big deal." We talked about it for twenty minutes. Fortunately, they believed me. I was relieved.

Months went by. I talked to three of my siblings and found out that he had abused them too. They had never forgotten the abuse. They just never talked about it before.

Taking On the Church

After I found out he'd abused my siblings as well, I wrote several letters to the bishop. My first concern was getting Father John away from other kids. The bishop's responses were cold and it was clear he wasn't going to take any action, so I decided to file a lawsuit against Father John and the diocese.

I filed in August 1991. Then I made copies of the lawsuit and Xeroxed his photo. I took a couple of days off from work and drove to half a dozen towns where he had served. I went to every newspaper and radio and TV station and talked to them.

The minute I went public, I started getting calls from people who'd been abused by a priest, by a brother, by a Catholic school teacher. I got an average of two calls a week. One was from another young man who'd been abused by Father Whiteley.

I knew I could have no control over the legal outcome, but if nothing else, people would read about the case, see his name, see his face, and maybe they would ask their kids if anything had ever happened to them. My goal was to make sure that he was removed from kids and to warn parents.

A year into my lawsuit, Father Whiteley vanished. They had moved him from a parish job to a desk job after I sued. Then, in 1993, my lawsuit was thrown out of the Missouri Supreme Court because of the statute of limitations.

Getting Involved in SNAP

At one point, my attorney suggested I get in touch with SNAP, Survivors Network of those Abused by Priests. The woman who answered the phone said all the right things. She listened to me and immediately said, "I'm terribly sorry about what happened to you. That must have been awful for you." And, "I've had those same feelings. I felt like it was my fault."

I got involved with SNAP and it constantly spurred me on to more activism. There's nothing like sitting around with thirty other people who've been mistreated by a priest or by a bishop to make you want to do something about it. As a kid I was powerless. I couldn't do a thing. Now I can.

I can't undo the past, but if I can help someone else heal a little bit faster or get a perpetrator removed from his post, that's the most I can hope for. If my efforts keep one other kid from being abused, then it's all been worth it.

I Loved My Father: Randi's Story

Randi Taylor is thirty years old.* She is single, lives alone, and works as a restaurant manager in Seattle. She was raised in an upper-middle-class white family of European descent. Randi has two sisters and two brothers.

Randi was always Daddy's girl. She idolized her father. The molestation began when Randi was twelve and continued for the next two years, just as she was going through puberty. It always was hidden in games and laughing.

I never saw anyone like me in the incest books. I never saw anyone who had a good relationship with her father. All the perpetrators looked like angry, ugly, mean people, and yet my father appeared to be a loving, charming, wonderful man. I loved and adored him. He treasured me.

---

* Randi Taylor wanted to use her own name but couldn't for legal reasons.

My father and I would do a lot of fun things together. I'd pour a glass of water on his head, and he'd pour a glass of water on mine. We'd be tickling and wrestling and chasing each other around the house. A lot of times when he was tickling me, he'd reach his hand around and cup my breast. I'd always scream at him not to do that, but my screams would get mixed up with all the laughter, hilarity, and screaming that was already going on. I'd tell him to stop and he'd say, "Oh, gee, did I slip? I didn't mean to." He made a mockery of it.

Whenever we rode in the car, I'd sit in the middle of the front seat. When we went around a sharp turn, my father would elbow my boobs. He'd do it on purpose, always with an exaggerated gesture. My sisters and I had a name for it. We said my father was "boobing" me.

Then there was a routine we went through every morning. I'd get up to brush my teeth. When I came back to my room I'd have to search in my closet or under my bed because my father would be hiding there, waiting for me to undress. I knew he wanted to see me naked. I'd have to chase him out. I had to protect myself from this Peeping Tom who was my father. But it was made into a game. It was just a normal part of the Taylor family morning routine.

At one point my father took up a sudden interest in photography, but he only wanted to photograph his daughters. He made me wear a thin T-shirt and he shined a light from behind my boobs. He wanted a picture of my boobs showing through a filmy T-shirt.

While he was doing the photos, his hands would get shaky. His breath would be louder than normal. He would be excited. It was very scary for me to see him that way. Here was this man I adored. He was out of control and I never knew how far he would go.

One time, my mother was going to be away all day. I was home sick from school. And in the middle of the day, my father came home from work. I was very frightened. I said, "What are you doing here?" He was joking and smiling and happy. "Oh, I thought I'd come home to see you. I knew you were here by yourself not feeling good."

He'd brought home some felt-tipped pens, and the game he had in mind was to decorate my breasts. He made me pull up my nightgown and he drew on my body. He made my two breasts into eyes, and then he drew a nose and mouth beneath it. His hands were shaking and his breath was really hot while he was doing that. And all the time, he was joking and teasing. It was horrible for me. Yet it was the one experience that allowed me to feel anger at him later on. All the rest of it, I said to myself, "Oh, he just slipped accidentally." But this was clearly thought out ahead of time. It was the only time he did anything that no one else saw him do. The rest of it was all out in the open.

I Didn't Know How to Say No

Before he molested me, I was a happy child. But after it happened, I started hanging out with guys with motorcycles, the kind of guys who drank a lot, had tattoos, and dropped out of school. I had a boyfriend who was a year older than me. I got pregnant the first time we had sex.

I was thirteen. I was afraid to tell my parents. I wore a lot of baggy clothes. I was six months pregnant before they figured it out. It shows how little parenting was going on. My mother and I went shopping for a new bra because my breasts were swelling. When she saw me nude in the dressing room, she knew, but she didn't say anything to me. She came home and told my father.

That night, when I was in bed, he came into my room and asked if I was pregnant. I said I was. He told me my mother had known I was pregnant because my breasts had changed, that the nipples were larger and the brown area around the nipples had gotten bigger and browner. Then he said he wanted to see. I protested. He said he wouldn't touch me, and he insisted that I pull up my shirt. He stared at my breasts for a few minutes, and then he let me pull my shirt down. I felt invaded and ashamed.

My parents never got angry at me for the pregnancy. They asked me what I wanted to do. I said I wanted to get rid of it. I flew to New York with my mother to some sleazy hospital for a saline abortion. The nurses had me give birth in a bedpan. It was only then that I realized it was a baby. It wasn't just a thing. I never found out if it was a girl or a boy.

My mother visited me a couple of times, but she only sat there crying. I ended up feeling guilty that I'd caused her all this pain. I felt like a horrible person. Once we got home, it was never mentioned again.

Why Was I Having Panic Attacks?

I started having anxiety attacks when I was a teenager, but they got really bad when I was in my twenties. They were crippling. Adrenaline would rush through my whole system. My muscles would pump up, my arms would tighten, my whole body would start to sweat and shake. My vision would change. It was like looking at an overexposed photo.

The panic attacks happened most frequently in the car. I'd be driving on the freeway and I'd feel like I was being forced to go faster than I wanted to go. When I had to pull up at a stoplight, I'd feel completely trapped. I'd want to run the red light.

One of my sisters is an alcoholic. When I was twenty-five, she got into AA and started reading books about incest. She came to me and said, "What Dad did to us was incest."

I said, "Maybe for you, but not for me. I love my father. He loves me. He never did anything to hurt me."

It took the longest time for me to believe that my experience counted. I felt that what happened to me was so minor compared to other women. My father just slipped once in a while.

I think it was the panic attacks—the fact that there was a direct result I could point to—that made me start to believe that he had done something wrong. They pushed me to break through that barrier of protecting my father, to face how terrified and angry I had been.

I finally made the connection. It was like a suspense thriller where the girl has trusted someone to protect her from the killer, and all of a sudden, she finds out he *is* the killer. My father, who was supposed to keep me safe from harm, *was* the harm.

For the first time in my life, I got angry at my father. He lost his hero status.

At First I Felt Sorry for My Father

My sister confronted my father a couple of years ago. When she told me she'd talked to him, I felt sorry for him. All I could think was, "How is he going to handle it?" I'd taken care of my father's emotional needs for so long that it was hard for me to recognize that he was a sick person who did bad things.

My father's admitted to me that what he did was wrong. He says I'm still special to him, and that the only important thing is that I get better. For a while he'd call me. I'd get angry at him and he'd apologize. But it wasn't really helping me. Finally I told him I didn't want to do that anymore.

Recently I wrote him a letter and said I didn't want to have any contact with him for the time being. I was crying, but it felt terrific to write. It's hard because I don't know what kind of relationship I will have with my father when this is all over. I don't know what will be left. But at least I know I'm getting healthy.

For Supporters of Survivors

"We have a much more fulfilling and exciting relationship than the one we started with. It's made us
close. I mean, you don't get close living in a bowl
of cherries."

Being a close supporter of a survivor healing from child sexual
abuse can be a tremendous challenge. Taking part in a deep healing
process can lead to real growth and closeness. But you may also feel
confused, scared, resentful, conflicted, isolated, or overwhelmed.
You may not know what to say, what to feel, or how to act. These
are natural responses to a difficult situation.

How to Help

When a survivor tells you "I was sexually abused," he or she is
entrusting you with something that is painful, frightening, and difficult to share. These guidelines can help you honor that trust and
support healing:

- **Believe the survivor.** Honor what the survivor is telling you.
- **Join with the survivor in validating the damage.** All abuse is harmful. Even if it's not violent, physical, or repeated, all abuse has serious consequences.
- **Be clear that abuse is never the child's fault.** Children ask for attention and affection. They do not ask for sexual abuse. Even if a child responds sexually, wasn't forced, or didn't protest, it is still never the child's fault. It is always the responsibility of the adult not to be sexual with a child.
- **Educate yourself about sexual abuse and the healing process.**
- **Don't sympathize with the abuser.** The survivor needs your total loyalty.
- **Validate the survivor's feelings of anger, pain, and fear.** These are natural, healthy responses to abuse. Survivors need to feel them, express them, and be heard.
- **Express your feelings.** If you have feelings of outrage, sympathy, or pain, share them. Just make sure they don't overpower the survivor's feelings.
- **Respect the time and space it takes to heal.** Healing is a slow process with lots of ups and downs. It can't be hurried.
- **Encourage the survivor to get help.** Survivors need a variety of support people to help them as they heal.
- **Get help if the survivor is suicidal.** Don't hesitate or try to deal with it alone. Get professional help. If you don't know whom else to call, ask the operator for the number for suicide prevention.
- **Accept that there will probably be changes in your relationship as the survivor heals.**
- **Resist seeing the survivor as a victim.** Continue to see the survivor as a strong, courageous human being struggling to resolve a major trauma.

Take Care of Yourself

Being involved with someone who is actively working through issues of child sexual abuse can be very demanding. This is a time when it's important to take care of yourself. Honor your own needs. If the survivor wants you to give more than you're able to give, admit your limits. Encourage the survivor to reach out to others. Take breaks.

Get help for yourself. Dealing with such raw pain is difficult. You need a place you can go to talk about your own fears, doubts, and frustrations.

One person's pain can sometimes bring up hurt for another. If you find yourself feeling extremely defensive or upset, seek help for dealing with your own unresolved pain.

National Child Abuse Hotline

Childhelp USA
1-800-422-4453
www.childhelpusa.org

This free twenty-four-hour hotline offers crisis counseling, help in finding a counselor or support group in your area, and information for both adults and children who have been abused. They also can tell you how to report abuse.

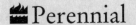 Perennial  Quill

Books by the authors:

THE COURAGE TO HEAL
A Guide for Women Survivors of Child Sexual Abuse
ISBN 0-06-095066-8 (paperback by Ellen Bass and Laura Davis) • ISBN 0-898-45833-1 (audio)
An inspiring, comprehensive guide that takes readers step-by-step through the healing process—changing their lives and convincing them that healing is possible.

THE COURAGE TO HEAL WORKBOOK
A Guide for Women Survivors of Child Sexual Abuse
ISBN 0-06-096437-5 (paperback by Laura Davis)
Using a combination of checklists, writing and art projects, open-ended questions, and activities, Davis expertly guides survivors through the healing process.

I NEVER TOLD ANYONE
Writings by Women Survivors of Child Sexual Abuse
ISBN 0-06-096573-8 (paperback edited by Ellen Bass and Louise Thornton)
A classic anthology of deeply moving testimonies by survivors of child sexual abuse.

BEGINNING TO HEAL (REVISED EDITION)
A First Book for Men and Women Who Were Sexually Abused As Children
ISBN 0-06-056469-5 (paperback by Ellen Bass and Laura Davis)
A clear, compassionate guide that takes readers by the hand and leads them through the first painful steps of healing from child sexual abuse.

ALLIES IN HEALING
When the Person You Love Is a Survivor of Child Sexual Abuse
ISBN 0-06-096883-4 (paperback by Laura Davis)
Practical advice and encouragement to all partners trying to support the survivors in their lives while tending to their own needs.

I THOUGHT WE'D NEVER SPEAK AGAIN
The Road from Estrangement to Reconciliation
ISBN 0-06-095702-6 (paperback by Laura Davis)
An emotional map of the process of reconciliation, guiding readers toward mending embittered relationships and fostering reconnection in place of estrangement.

FREE YOUR MIND
The Book for Gay, Lesbian, and Bisexual Youth—and Their Allies
ISBN 0-06-095104-4 (paperback by Ellen Bass and Kate Kaufman)
Alive with the voices of more than fifty young people, *Free Your Mind* addresses the issues facing gay youth and provides detailed guidance for supportive adults.